learn live it
learn

BIBLE STUDIES

CHRISTIAN CHARACTER

Group
Loveland, Colorado
www.group.com

Group resources actually work!

This Group resource helps you focus on **"The 1 Thing™"**— a life-changing relationship with Jesus Christ. "The 1 Thing" incorporates our **R.E.A.L.** approach to ministry. It reinforces a growing friendship with Jesus, encourages long-term learning, and results in life transformation, because it's:

Relational
Learner-to-learner interaction enhances learning and builds Christian friendships.

Experiential
What learners experience through discussion and action sticks with them up to 9 times longer than what they simply hear or read.

Applicable
The aim of Christian education is to equip learners to be both hearers and doers of God's Word.

Learner-based
Learners understand and retain more when the learning process takes into consideration how they learn best.

Credits
Contributors: Karl Leuthauser, Keith Madsen, K.C. Mason, A. Koshy Muthalaly, and Lori Niles
Editor: Beth Robinson
Development Editor: Matt Lockhart
Chief Creative Officer: Joani Schultz
Copy Editor: Loma Huh
Art Directors: Jean Bruns and Joyce Douglas
Cover Art Director: Jeff A. Storm
Cover Designer: Toolbox Creative
Cover Photographer: Rodney Stewart
Print Production Artist: Pat Miller
Production Manager: Dodie Tipton

Unless otherwise noted, Scripture taken from the HOLY BIBLE, NEW INTERNATIONAL VERSION®. Copyright © 1973, 1978, 1984 by International Bible Society. Used by permission of Zondervan Publishing House. All rights reserved.

ISBN 0-7644-2776-8
10 9 8 7 6 5 4 3 2 1   13 12 11 10 09 08 07 06 05

Printed in the United States of America.

Contents

Introduction to Group's
Learn It, Live It Bible Studies®

Welcome to an exciting new concept in small-group Bible studies! At Group, we recognize the value of Bible study to Christian growth—there's no better way to grow in our faith than to study the living Word of God. We also know the value of group activity. Activity helps us practice what we learn, and this is vital to the Christian faith. Jesus didn't tell us to simply learn about him; he asks us to become like him in thoughts, in words, and in actions. That's why Group developed *Learn It, Live It Bible Studies*®. In these studies, you'll be challenged not only to learn more about God but also to put what you've learned into practice in a powerful and meaningful way.

Whether you're new to Bible study or a seasoned pro, you'll find each lesson's Bible study to be interesting and compelling. You'll open God's Word with the others in your group. You'll study relevant Scripture passages and discuss thought-provoking questions that will help you all grow in your faith and in your understanding of who God is and what he wants for your lives.

After the Bible study, you'll be invited to choose a group project that will help you practice the very thing you've just learned. Some of these projects are simple, easy, and low-risk. Others will require a greater commitment of time and resources; they may even take you beyond your comfort zone. But whichever group project you choose to do, you can be certain that it will help you grow more like Christ in your everyday life.

We hope you enjoy these lessons! And we pray that by studying these lessons and doing these projects, you'll find yourself becoming more and more like our Lord Jesus Christ.

Christian Character

This eight-session Bible study focuses on helping Christ-followers develop Christian character. To develop character is to learn to live our values in such a way that they characterize our very being. It's one thing to believe in the importance of perseverance—it's a wholly different thing to be a person who consistently perseveres. It isn't easy to live out our faith in this way, to be molded into the image of Christ. It requires that we let go of ingrained habits and long-held attitudes that neither benefit us nor honor God.

Yet the moment we devote our lives to God, he begins the process of conforming our character to his. While the Holy Spirit is the agent of change in our lives, we have an important role in the process. Through study, practice, and submission to God's will and work in our lives, we become Christlike in our attitudes and actions. The sessions in this study will help you learn about and practice eight character traits that are important in the Christian life. May these sessions help you to grow in appreciation, love, and devotion to God. And may these sessions also help you become more like Jesus with each passing day.

About the Sessions

Part 1: *learn it*

Start It *(15 minutes)*

This part of the lesson is designed to introduce everyone to the day's topic and to get your discussion flowing. Here you'll find an introduction to read over and a quick warm-up activity to do together, along with a few discussion questions.

Study It *(45-60 minutes)*

This is the Bible study portion of the lesson. Every lesson provides several Scripture passages to look up and eight to twelve discussion questions for you to talk over as a group. Feel free to jot down your insights in the space provided.

You'll also notice that each lesson includes extra information in the margins. You'll find statistics, Bible facts, definitions, and quotations. Please note that the information doesn't always come from a Christian perspective. These notes are meant to be thought-provoking and to get your group discussing each topic at a deeper level.

Close It *(15-30 minutes)*

During the Close It section of the lesson, you'll do two things. First, you'll read through the Live It options at the end of the lesson and choose one to do together as a group. You'll find more information about the Live It options in the next section.

Second, you'll pray together as a group. Be sure to take the time to listen to each other's prayer requests. You may want to write those prayer requests in the space provided so you can pray for those requests throughout the week. Don't rush your time with God. Praying with others is a precious opportunity—make the most of it!

Part 2: live it

In each lesson in this study, you'll find five Live It options. These group activities are designed to help your Bible study group live out what you learned in the Bible study. Together as a group, read over the Live It options each week. Then choose one to do together. You'll find that some of the activities are quick and easy and can be easily done without planning an extra session. While other activities will require more time and planning. Some activities are very low-risk; others might push group members to the edge of their comfort zone. Some of the activities are suitable for entire families to participate in; others will work better if you arrange for child care. Choose the option that interests your group the most and carry it out. You'll find that you learn so much more when you practice it in real life.

Courage

"We shall fight in France. We shall fight on the seas and oceans. We shall fight with growing confidence and growing strength in the air. We shall defend our island whatever the cost may be...We shall fight in the fields and in the streets...We shall never surrender!"

Winston Churchill was one of the only voices in the world courageous enough to cry out against Hitler's war machine. Through the initial courage of one cantankerous Englishman and the thousands who followed his call, the menacing world power of the late 1930s was held at bay until the resistance of the Soviet Union and the untapped resources of the United States came to England's aid. Would the outcome of World War II have been the same if Winston Churchill had acquiesced in cowardice to Hitler as his predecessor Neville Chamberlain had done?

One person's courage *can* make a world of difference. In the face of tyrants, social ills, or another person's pain, it is so easy to do nothing—to simply wish for the best while bemoaning the state of the world. But God calls us to so much more. We are to be the voice that calls out in darkness, pointing the way to freedom, life, and truth. If we face our fears and muster our courage, we *will* change our world.

Part 1: *learn it*

Start It *(15 minutes)*

Foiling Phobias

Leader: Because this is the start of a new study series (or perhaps it's the first meeting of your small group), take the opportunity to help group members discuss their expectations for the series and the relationships in the group. You might consider having the members draft a list of expectations for the group, such as attendance and how long the meeting should be.

Leader: Gather paper and pens for this activity.

Give everyone a pencil and a piece of paper. Have someone in your group read the following three paragraphs aloud:

You've probably heard of acrophobia, the fear of heights. And perhaps you're familiar with aerophobia and agoraphobia, the fear of air and the fear of public places, respectively. Apparently, there are many other paralyzing fears that have their own unique names. According to various online phobia lists, there's a name for the fear of looking up, anablephobia. Arachibutyrophobia is said to be the fear of peanut butter sticking to the roof of the mouth. The lists say that if you have bromidrosiphobia, you're afraid of body smells. Ironically, www.phobialist.com names hippopotomonstrosesquippedaliophobia as the fear of long words.

While the latter phobias may or may not find their way into medical or psychological journals, chances are that someone suffers from those fears. On your slip of paper, create a name for an abnormal fear you have. Perhaps you live in Nebraska and you won't go swimming because of your fear of sharks. If you can't think of a fear, create a word for a pet peeve or discomfort you're especially sensitive to. For example, maybe the sound of a bell choir makes your head ring.

Then write a sentence or two that succinctly describes a time in your life when you feel you displayed courage.

Put all of the slips of paper in the middle of the group. Have each person draw one and try to guess who it belongs to. If time allows, after each person's identity is revealed, give him or her the opportunity to share more about the fear and the act of courage. Then discuss the following questions:

- **What surprised you most about each other's "phobias"?**

- **Why are some people overly sensitive or fearful of things that don't seem to bother others?**

- **Which courageous act did you find especially moving or interesting?**

Study It *(45-60 minutes)*

> **If you have a large group, form smaller groups of four to seven people to answer the discussion questions. At the end of the Study It section, allow time for the subgroups to report to the whole group.**

Read Joshua 1:9.

1. What do you think courage is and where do you think it comes from?

2. Why is courage necessary or desirable in the life of a Christian?

Read the quote in the margin.

3. How did Martin Luther King's experiences in life give him such a profound understanding of the relationship between courage and fear? How have your own experiences in life shaped your understanding of courage and cowardice?

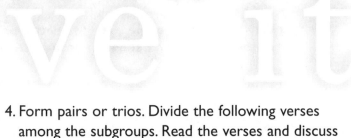

> "Courage is an inner resolution to go forward in spite of obstacles and frightening situations; cowardice is a submissive surrender to circumstance. Courage breeds creative self-affirmation; cowardice produces destructive self-abnegation. Courage faces fear and thereby masters it; cowardice represses fear and is thereby mastered by it."
>
> **—Martin Luther King Jr.,** *Strength to Love*

4. Form pairs or trios. Divide the following verses among the subgroups. Read the verses and discuss what they have to say about courage. After a couple minutes, have the pairs or trios summarize their verses and share their insights with the rest of the group.

- *Genesis 3:6-12*
- *Psalm 27:1-3*
- *Psalm 118:6-9*

- *Daniel 3:13-18*
- *Philippians 1:12-20*

Read 1 Samuel 13:23–14:1, 14:6-15.

5. Why do you think Jonathan had such confidence that God would save them? What has God done in your past that gives you courage for your future?

6. Why do you think Jonathan's armor-bearer had such confidence and courage? Describe a time when you had to entrust your fate into someone else's hands? When do you ever find that it's hard to trust your leaders? to trust God?

Read the song lyrics in the margin.

7. What part does the "prince of darkness" have in causing us to lose courage? Why would it be a victory for our enemy to cause *you* to lose courage?

And tho' this world, with devils filled, Should threaten to undo us, We will not fear, for God hath willed His truth to triumph thru us. The prince of darkness grim— We tremble not for him; His rage we can endure, For lo! his doom is sure— One little word shall fell him.

—**Martin Luther, "A Mighty Fortress Is Our God"**

8. How can we overcome obstacles and stay strong in our courage?

9. Is there ever a time when courage is foolhardy—when it's right to be hesitant or even fearful? What's the proper balance between caution and courage?

10. What difference can being a person of courage make in your life? How can you grow in courage?

Close It (15-30 minutes)

Review the options in the Live It section of this session and make plans as a group to complete one of these activities prior to moving on to the next session. This is your opportunity to move from theory to practice—*carpe diem!*

Pray It

Share prayer requests and close in prayer. Be sure to ask God to guide your efforts as you plan and carry out a Live It activity.

Plan It

What activity are we going to do?

When are we doing this?

Where will this take place?

Other: special instructions/my responsibility

Part 2: live it

Option 1

Plan a time of courageous worship. Work together to find songs, Scripture passages, and stories of triumph that give you courage in the midst of trouble or fear. Begin your time with singing all of the verses to Martin Luther's "A Mighty Fortress Is Our God." Then sing together the other songs you've collected and share the Scripture passages and stories. Be sure to en*courage* each other and to spend time in prayer, praising and thanking God for the courage he gives.

Option 2

With a partner from the group, identify a fear you have that hinders your effectiveness in advancing God's kingdom. Tell your partner your fear. Pray together, and then come up with a list of very small steps you can take toward overcoming that fear. For example, if you are afraid to tell people about Christ, your first step might be to introduce yourself to your neighbor. From there you could invite your neighbor over for a barbecue. You could continue to purposefully build a relationship with your neighbor until your neighbor asks you about your faith or a natural opportunity presents itself. Make sure that the steps you plan are things you can begin to do this week. Get started on the steps and see how far you get. Then, when the group gets back together, plan to spend some time talking about how everyone did in courageously overcoming his or her fear. Be sure to encourage each other and pray together.

Option 3

Choose an outreach project or event for which everyone in the room admits at least a minor level of discomfort. Avoid projects that strike terror into everyone's hearts or serve as a poor reflection of what your group is about. Service projects for people who are "different" are a great place to start. Here are some ideas: Plan a Saturday morning of activities for children in a homeless shelter. Plan to spend an evening visiting and praying with senior citizens at a nursing home. Visit several people who've visited your church and tell them more about Jesus and the church. Before the project, talk candidly about your fears or misgivings. Brainstorm ways to make the experience more comfortable or accessible, and then face your fears!

Option 4

Plan an outdoor adventure for your group! Put together a one-day event or overnight retreat that includes an adrenaline-pumping experience. You may choose to go white-water rafting, horseback riding, race-car driving, rock climbing, or even skydiving. Make certain your group uses a highly qualified professional guide on your adventure and that no one feels pressured to participate. After the event, share how the experience was similar to or different from having courage in daily life.

Option 5

Take a courageous stand for Christ in your community. Is there an injustice or immoral practice that's tolerated in your community? Together, write letters to city officials and to the editor of your local newspaper. Make personal appointments with city council members or even the mayor to talk about your concerns. Find out how to get on the agenda at a city council meeting and present your concerns publicly. You could even publish fliers about your concerns to hand out at local fairs and festivals or door-to-door.

Debrief It

After experiencing this session's Live It activity, discuss these questions as a group:

- **On a scale of 1 (low) to 10 (high), how would you rank this experience for yourself? Why?**

- **What was the most important insight you gained from this experience?**

- **How can you further develop this character trait?**

Journal It

The following space is provided for you to record your personal thoughts, reflections, impressions or feelings about this session's topic and Live It activity.

Compassion

Our call to be compassionate comes from Jesus' words in Matthew 25:40: " 'I tell you the truth, whatever you did for one of the least of these brothers of mine, you did for me.' " Mother Teresa, who exemplified a life of compassion, called this the "Gospel on Five Fingers: You-Did-It-To-Me." Can we imagine passing Christ, leaving him hungry, thirsty, or lacking clothes? Yet we routinely pass by those whose needs overwhelm us, failing to remember that Christ didn't call us to solve the problems of the world, only to act in compassion.

Compassion benefits others, but because true compassion means sharing of another's circumstances, we ourselves are blessed in the process. Our experience is enlarged, and we come to know Christ more deeply and fully by identifying with those he identifies himself with. How that happens, exactly, is a mystery. That it happens is well documented throughout Christian history as we see the face of Christ in those who lack resources of every kind.

Philip Yancey, in his book *What's So Amazing About Grace*, says, "The Christian knows to serve the weak not because they deserve it but because God extended his love to us when we deserved the opposite." Serving the weak in compassion extends the circle of God's love to us back to him. As your small group learns about the many facets of compassion, you'll be challenged to reach deep inside yourselves to love God through loving the unlovely and through loving those who are dear to you with a more tender mercy when they may seem to deserve the opposite.

Start It (*15 minutes*)

Broken Hearts

> **Leader:** Before this session make or purchase enough large paper hearts for each pair or trio to have one. You'll also need tape.
>
> **Leader:** Form pairs or trios for this hands-on activity. Gather the group back together when it is time to discuss the questions.

Share with your partners something that breaks your heart, tearing a piece from the paper heart as you do so. When everyone in your group has shared one or two things, use tape to put the heart back together.

Then discuss the following questions with the whole group:

- **You've shared the things that break your hearts. How do you think God feels about these things?**

- **What was your experience in trying to bring wholeness back to the heart? How is that like or unlike your attempts to do something about the things that break your heart?**

- **How do you feel when your attempts to bring healing are unsuccessful? are successful?**

Study It (*45-60 minutes*)

> If you have a large group, form smaller groups of four to seven people to answer the discussion questions. At the end of the Study It section, allow time for the subgroups to report to the whole group.

Read Ephesians 4:32–5:2.

1. What do these verses say about the relationship between our compassion and Christ's work on our behalf?

2. What is it that makes it difficult to act with compassion toward those in situations that break our hearts? What makes it easier?

> "It is only pride and selfishness and coldness that keep us from having compassion. When we ultimately go home to God, we are going to be judged on what we were to each other, what we did for each other, and, especially, how much love we put in that. It's not how much we give, but how much love we put in the doing—that's compassion in action."
>
> —Mother Teresa

Read the quotation in the margin.

3. How have you seen pride, selfishness, or coldness get in the way of compassion? What else have you observed getting in the way of someone acting in compassion?

Read Luke 15:17-24.

4. What did the father in the story set aside in order to show compassion? What did he invest? What lessons for us are in this example of compassion?

In Scripture, a number of different words can be translated "compassion." In the Old Testament, you will find:

- *chamal*—to commiserate or spare (Exodus 2:6)
- *racham*—an earthy image, meaning to fondle or hold lovingly (2 Kings 13:23)

In the New Testament, you will find:

- *splagchnizomai*—to be moved with feeling for suffering (Matthew 9:36)
- *oikteiro*—to exercise pity (Romans 9:15)
- *metriopatheo*—to be gentle or to treat indulgently (Hebrews 5:2)
- *sumpathes*—having a shared feeling (of pain) (Hebrews 10:34)
- *eleeo*—to have mercy on (Jude 22)

Read the margin note about different types of compassion.

5. What's the relationship between feeling and action in compassion?

6. Form pairs or trios. Divide the following verses among the subgroups. Read the verses and discuss Jesus' experiences with compassion. After a couple minutes, have the pairs or trios summarize their verses and share their insights with the rest of the group.

- *Matthew 9:36*
- *Matthew 14:13-14*
- *Matthew 15:29-32*
- *Matthew 20:29-34*
- *Mark 1:40-42*

7. What inspired Jesus' compassion? What do Jesus' responses to the people he had compassion on tell us about how we can respond to those who inspire our compassion?

> "Those who unlock your compassion are those to whom you have been assigned."
>
> —Unknown

Read the quote in the margin and 2 Corinthians 1:3-7.

8. What is your response to the concept of Christians being "assigned" on the basis of a sense of compassion? Is a sense of compassion a reliable source on which to base compassionate action? Why or why not?

Read Philippians 2:1-4 and Colossians 3:12.

9. How does having a clear sense of receiving God's compassion influence your decisions on a daily basis?

Close It *(15-30 minutes)*

Review the options in the Live It section of this session and make plans as a group to complete one of these activities prior to moving on to the next session. This is your opportunity to move from theory to practice—*carpe diem!*

Pray It

Share prayer requests and close in prayer. Be sure to ask God to guide your efforts as you plan and carry out a Live It activity.

Plan It

What activity are we going to do?

When are we doing this?

Where will this take place?

Other: special instructions/my responsibility

Part 2: live it

Option 1

Together, shop for and assemble nonperishable compassion sacks to carry in your cars. Include a juice or water bottle, an energy bar or vacuum-sealed chicken or tuna salad pack, a cup of fruit, and a pudding snack along with a napkin and plastic utensils. You may also want to include personal hygiene items such as shampoo, toothpaste, and a toothbrush. Include a New Testament, along with information on how to have a relationship with Jesus. Covenant together to overcome whatever hesitancy you might have to reach out with compassion by giving these gifts to hungry or homeless people as you encounter them.

Option 2

For one entire day, agree to do all your tasks with the "great love" referred to in the quotation from Mother Teresa (p. 21). Strive to do the household chores, care for your children, drive your car, do your job, deal with your co-workers, and run your errands all with the love and compassion that our faith in God calls us to. Throughout the day, stop and repeat these words from Jonah 4:2: "I knew that you are a compassionate God, slow to anger and abounding in love." Recall why it's important to be compassionate and loving in your actions and attitudes and redirect yourself. In your next meeting, share how that reminder of the nature of God impacted your attitudes.

Option 3

Work with the social service agencies in your community or talk to the leaders of your church to find a person or a family who could use loving, compassionate care. Together, find out what they need and supply it. Perhaps you could care for an elderly person's yard for several months. Perhaps there's a single mother who needs after-school care for her children. As you look around for a project, here are some guidelines: Make sure that you serve people rather than causes or agencies. Choose a project where you can be involved over a period of time. Choose a project where you can get involved in someone's life.

Option 4

Go someplace in your community where people gather, such as a shopping center, a university, a sporting complex, or a festival. Simply spend an hour or two watching people and praying for them. Ask God to help you see the needs around you and the people around you through eyes of compassion. Ask God to show you how your group can serve your community with compassion. The needs of the heart are often more difficult to spot than the needs of the physical realm. After you complete your observations, compare your impressions and discuss the responses you might have to the needs you observed as a group. Be sure to follow through by planning ways your group can meet the needs you saw.

Option 5

The National Hunger Clearinghouse (http://www.world hungeryear.org/nhc_data/nhc_01.asp) can help you find organizations in local communities that address a variety of human needs. Just enter your town, state, and ZIP code to locate food distribution centers, gleaning opportunities, nutrition education programs, and economic development programs near you. Look at the possible ways you can join with your community to represent Christ through compassionate cooperation.

Debrief It

After experiencing this session's Live It activity, discuss these questions as a group:

- **On a scale of 1 (low) to 10 (high), how would you rank this experience for yourself? Why?**

- **What was the most important insight you gained from this experience?**

- **How can you further develop this character trait?**

The following space is provided for you to record your personal thoughts, reflections, impressions, or feelings about this session's topic and Live It activity.

Integrity

Integrity can be hard to accurately define, though we easily recognize it when we see a person who has a strong sense of integrity. It's even easier to recognize a lack of integrity in an individual or an institution. Integrity is not so much a value itself as the sense of completeness that comes when we live up to our values. Integrity is walking our talk, and doing so with conviction. People who manifest integrity stir our soul. Integrity is Jimmy Stewart as Mr. Smith in *Mr. Smith Goes to Washington*, standing up, filibustering for what is right until he collapses. Integrity is Erin Brockovich fighting for the rights of the underdog against a big, powerful corporation.

In contrast to these examples of strong integrity, in the movie *Hook*, Robin Williams plays a grown-up Peter Pan who has forgotten his identity and become a ruthless lawyer. He keeps making promises to his son that he later breaks. He says, "My word is my bond," but the son soon decides that his father's word is at best a "junk bond." What a poignant lesson!

Don't you find that you want to be around the kind of people who stand for the truth at all costs? And don't you want to *be* that kind of person? God calls us to walk in integrity. This lesson will help you explore how to do that.

Part 1: *learn it*

Start It *(15 minutes)*

Reputations

Together, brainstorm names of famous people. After each name is called out, have everyone vote thumbs up (the person has integrity) or thumbs down (the person lacks integrity). Keep brainstorming until you've mentioned at least thirty people. If there's a difference of opinion about whether the person has integrity or not, have people explain why they voted the way they did. After you're finished brainstorming, discuss these questions:

- **How has integrity or the lack of it affected the lives of these famous people?**

- **How important is it to have integrity?**

- **Why does society care about integrity?**

Study It *(30-45 minutes)*

> **Leader: If you have a large group, form smaller groups of four to seven people to answer the discussion questions. At the end of the Study It section, allow time for the smaller groups to report to the whole group.**

1. What is integrity? Why is integrity important to God?

2. When have you been disappointed by a person with little integrity?

3. When have you seen the cause of Christ harmed by those with little integrity?

4. Form pairs or trios. Have each pair or trio look up one of the following Scripture passages and note what it teaches about integrity. After a few minutes, have each pair or trio summarize its passage and share insights with the rest of the group.

- *Psalm 112:4-8*
- *Daniel 6:1-23*
- *Matthew 5:33-37*
- *Luke 16:1-15*

Read Acts 5:1-11.

5. In what ways can a lack of integrity destroy or harm a person?

6. What role does integrity play in the relationships between Christians? in the relationships between Christians and non-Christians?

> "We are all constrained to balance what we actually are with the image we want to display. We learn to bridge this gap by self-delusion ('I really believe this must be true') or by rationalization ('I didn't mean to say that, and besides, it didn't do any harm'). But if we aspire to grow as human beings, we should struggle to close the gap by making our inner selves truer reflections of our own highest values."
>
> —Jimmy Carter, *Living Faith*

Read the margin quotation.

7. Why do you think we have such a strong temptation toward self-delusion and rationalization? How do these tendencies interfere with our efforts to be people of integrity?

8. What do you see as the most important step in making your inner self a "truer reflection of your own highest values"?

Read I John 1:5-7.

9. What specifically can you do to become a person whose inner self and outer self radiate the light of integrity and Christlike values?

Close It *(15-30 minutes)*

Review the options in the Live It section of this session and make plans as a group to complete one of these activities prior to moving on to the next session. This is your opportunity to move from theory to practice—*carpe diem!*

Pray It

Share prayer requests and close in prayer. Be sure to ask God to guide your efforts as you plan and carry out a Live It activity.

Plan It

What activity are we going to do?

When are we doing this?

Where will this take place?

Other: special instructions/my responsibility

Option 1

Have everyone do an "integrity audit" of their checking account or credit card account. As you review your records, ask the basic question, "Does what I spend money on reflect what I say my values are?" If you say that you value caring for people more than you value things, how many of your checks go toward caring for people? How many checks can you find that went for things you are not proud of? For example, you may spend money on cigarettes when you'd like to quit smoking; or you may spend too much money on hobbies, recreation, or restaurant meals when your values indicate that more of your money should be spent on charity. If you were to give yourself a grade (A through F) for how well your checkbook reflects your values, what grade would it be? Discuss the insights you've gained with the others in the group.

Option 2

What does it mean to be a *church* that operates with integrity? As a group, compile a list of issues that are relevant to whether a church is operating with integrity. Included might be issues like these: Does it pay a responsible wage to those in its employ? Does it give members opportunities to act on what the church teaches? For example, if your church values helping people make a commitment to follow Jesus, does it actively evangelize in the community and does it train its members to share their faith with others? Design a "Church Integrity Test" based on biblical values and then evaluate your church. Make sure this doesn't turn into an opportunity to find fault or to nitpick. If there are areas where your church doesn't live what it preaches, prayerfully consider whether the members in your group are being called by God to organize programs in those areas.

Option 3

Have each member of the group come up with a mission statement for his or her life. Then have each group member write down five to seven core values that will help him or her fulfill that mission. Have everyone meet with a partner to compare mission statements and core values. When you meet with your partner, honestly discuss to what degree your life matches your values. Discuss these questions: Do you plan or dream to live a certain way, but find your real life never meets your ideals? To what extent is this an integrity issue?

Come up with several practical things you can do to live your life according to your values and your mission. Choose at least one thing you can do this week. For example, maybe you'd like to talk about your faith with your children or your neighbors more. Maybe you'd like to live by biblical money management principles, or perhaps you'd like to allow God to control your daily decisions. Pray together with your partner, asking God's help to live your life with more integrity. Call, e-mail, or meet with your partner several times throughout the week. Offer each other accountability and encouragement.

Option 4

Reread the quotation from Jimmy Carter (p. 32). Together, consider where your inside life doesn't match up with the image you show the world. Take fifteen minutes to quietly reflect on your own life and consider where you employ self-delusion or rationalization. Write down ways that you portray a more "put together" or successful image to the world than what you really are. Then, as much as you feel comfortable, confess your real self to the others in the group. Discuss how you can all "close the gap by making [your] inner selves truer reflections of [your] own highest values." Then have each person in the group choose one specific thing he or she can do this week to lead a more authentic life. Throughout the week, encourage each other with prayer, e-mails, and phone calls to live lives of integrity.

Option 5

Compile a list of all the moral instructions you have given to your children in the past couple of weeks. You may even want to ask them which ones they remember you saying to them. If there are other adults in the house, like a spouse or an in-law, ask them which ones they remember you telling your children. Then for the next week make yourself a scorecard for how many times you act out a teaching you have given your children, and how many times you act contrary to such a teaching. Where are you living out your values well, and where do you need some work?

Debrief It

After experiencing this week's Live It activity, discuss these questions as a group:

- **On a scale of 1 (low) to 10 (high), how would you rank this experience for yourself? Why?**

- **What was the most important insight you gained from this experience?**

- **How can you further develop this character trait?**

Journal It

The following space is provided for you to record your personal thoughts, reflections, impressions, or feelings about this session's topic and Live It activity.

Perseverance

Life, like a highway under construction, is filled with roadblocks and detours. Perseverance is what gets us to our destination, despite the challenges.

Perseverance has both an active and a passive quality. Sometimes, persevering means waiting through the traffic, and sometimes it means finding another way around. Always, we must be intentional in keeping the destination in mind. In Scripture, we're reminded again and again that our final destination is heaven and that the goal of spiritual perseverance is to dwell eternally unfettered in the presence of God, all roadblocks set aside.

Between our present location and our eternal destination, however, we can expect to encounter challenges that put us on the edge. Perseverance is not a stand-alone character trait. It is part of a continuum that starts with faith, goodness, knowledge, and self-control. It is followed by godliness, brotherly kindness, and love (2 Peter 1:5-8). Far from being a yoke of bondage, these character traits set us free to be effective and productive in the Christian life. As your small group learns about the concept of perseverance, you can encourage each other to hold on to what God has accomplished in your lives, so that you can reach forward to all that is to come.

Part 1: *learn it*

Start It *(15 minutes)*

Never Give Up

Have everyone in the group try this balancing pose.

Stand up and place the bottom of one foot on the inside of your other leg so that your raised knee is pointing out to the side. Then close your eyes. Hold the pose for at least thirty seconds. If you lose your balance, try again. Keep trying this for two or three minutes. Warmly congratulate anyone who is able to keep their balance for thirty seconds.

Then discuss the following questions:

- **What made this a frustrating activity?**

- **Did you find it easy to persevere? Why or why not? In real life, what makes it hard or easy to persevere?**

- **Tell about a time in your life when you persevered.**

Study It *(45-60 minutes)*

> If you have a large group, form smaller groups of four to seven people to answer the discussion questions. At the end of the Study It section, allow time for the subgroups to report to the whole group.

In the King James Version of the Bible, the word *perseverance* is often translated as "patience" (Romans 5:3-4 and 2 Thessalonians 3:5).

Read the margin note and look up the verses listed.

1. From your perspective, how are perseverance and patience similar? different?

2. Together, list some other words that you associate with the concept of perseverance. What do you think it means to persevere? Why does perseverance matter in the life of a Jesus-follower?

"O Lord God, when thou givest to thy servants to endeavour any great matter, grant us also to know that it is not the beginning, but the continuing of the same until it be thoroughly finished, which yieldeth the true glory."

—The Prayer of Sir Francis Drake

Read the Prayer of Sir Francis Drake.

3. Think about your own "great matters" in the life of faith. What is difficult about the idea of "continuing of the same"?

Read 1 Corinthians 9:24-27; Galatians 5:7; and Hebrews 12:1-6.

4. In what ways is perseverance like or unlike a race?

Read Job 17:6-9.

5. What circumstances did Job persevere under? What does Job's example say to our lives?

6. What are the hardest circumstances you've ever had to persevere under? What, in retrospect, are the benefits to your life today?

> "*Perseverance*...is the capacity to stick with the course, to stay with it over the long haul, regardless of how you may feel."
>
> "Character is...transformed by the process of perseverance under God."
>
> —Dallas Willard, *Renovation of the Heart*

Read the Dallas Willard quotations in the margin.

7. Do you agree with Willard that perseverance is sticking to something regardless of feelings? How does our attitude, either positive or negative, affect our perseverance?

Read the last two sentences of the introduction to this session (p. 39).

8. What does perseverance set us free from?

Read James 1:2-4 and 2 Peter 1:3-9.

9. How have you seen perseverance shaping your character? the character of others? What do you see as the role of perseverance in maturity?

Close It *(15-30 minutes)*

Review the options in the Live It section of this session and make plans as a group to complete one of these activities prior to moving on to the next session. This is your opportunity to move from theory to practice—*carpe diem!*

Pray It

Share prayer requests and close in prayer. Be sure to ask God to guide your efforts as you plan and carry out a Live It activity.

Plan It

What activity are we going to do?

When are we doing this?

Where will this take place?

Other: special instructions/my responsibility

Option 1

Rent the movie *Rudy* to watch together as a group. Discuss how the story of Rudy Ruettiger demonstrates perseverance. Share other real-life stories of endurance that have influenced your lives.

Next, choose a personal goal. It could be losing weight, finishing your degree, cleaning out the garage, having a consistent prayer time, organizing your cupboards, or reading all the way through the Bible this year. Talk together in your small group about your goal and what it will take to achieve it. Then get started—no excuses! In fact, write down any excuses you might come up with, and have the group help you come up with a strategy to over-come each excuse.

Start today on your goal. If it's worth doing, it's worth doing today! Do a little bit each day to achieve your goal. Persevere! At the end of the week, talk about your progress as well as any hur-dles you faced. Talk about why perseverance is hard, but also talk about the value of sticking to your plan. Encourage each other. Continue to check in with each other as you persevere toward achieving your goals.

Option 2

Fasting is a great way to develop perseverance. Choose a day this week to fast from food, sugar, television, or the Internet. If you're fasting from television or the Internet, the fast could last all week. Use the time you would have spent eating or watching television to pray, read Scripture, or spend time with your family. At the end of the week, get together and talk about your experiences. Was perse-vering worth it? What obstacles or challenges did you encounter? Did you develop strategies to help you stick to your plan? How will you apply your newfound perseverance to other areas of your life?

Option 3

Visit www.jesusvideo.org. This organization is dedicated to put-ting a video of Jesus' life and ministry in every home in America.

Your group can get involved. Learn about the project on the Web site. Then distribute videos in your own hometown. Prayerfully decide how much money the group can invest (it costs about $5 for each video) and how much of your town you'd like to reach. Then order the videos and prayerfully distribute them to homes in your community. You will likely find that bringing your vision to reality requires perseverance. Consider how you might raise funds to fulfill your project. Persevere as you walk through the streets of your community distributing videos to each home.

Option 4

Choose a spiritually challenging activity for the week that will require great discipline and perseverance. For example, perhaps there's a Christian book that you'd all like to read, or perhaps you'd like to commit to getting up at 5 a.m. every day of the week to pray for an hour or more. Choose a task for the group to do. Then persevere during the week. At the end of the week, get together and compare your experiences. What was easy? What was hard? Were you able to faithfully persevere? Was there benefit in perseverance? When is perseverance important? Are there times when it doesn't matter? Why is perseverance an admirable character trait for Christians?

Option 5

Choose a high-endurance activity to do together, such as a long, challenging hike. The hike must be long enough to challenge all members of the group, but still be doable. Be sure to plan for all contingencies: Take food, water, protective clothing, a first-aid kit, and whatever else you need in order to be safe. As you hike, pay attention to your emotions as you begin, along the way of the hike, and when you and the rest of the group all reach the goal. When you are finished, share the feelings you experienced and how these experiences provide a model for other occasions that require perseverance in your lives.

Debrief It

After experiencing this session's Live It activity, discuss these questions as a group:

- **On a scale of 1 (low) to 10 (high), how would you rank this experience for yourself? Why?**

- **What was the most important insight you gained from this experience?**

- **How can you further develop their character trait?**

Journal It

The following space is provided for you to record your personal thoughts, reflections, impressions, or feelings about this session's topic and Live It activity.

Humility

In many ways, humility is a virtue that's in direct opposition to the virtues promoted by the world in which we live. Today, the prevailing wisdom is that people need to have self-esteem, a strong self-image, and an almost cocky belief in the power of the individual to conquer all obstacles. Our children are taught that they are free to be themselves, and that if they can dream it, they can be it. There is nothing outside the realm of possibilities for a human being who simply has the attitude, "I think I can, I think I can."

The elevation of humanity in this way is opposed to the Christian virtue of humility. The Bible teaches that to have an accurate picture of who we are, we must have an accurate picture of who God is. Compared to a morally perfect being with the knowledge and power to create all we see, know, and experience with his words, we aren't much to brag about. Being properly humble means recognizing that all we are and all that we can become is a gift from our Creator who loves us enough to sacrifice his Son to give us eternal life.

Start It *(15 minutes)*

Positive or Negative

Find a partner and share stories from your life using the following discussion starters:

- Tell about a time when you were overly proud and it got you into trouble.

- Tell about a time when your own lack of pride or self-confidence caused trouble for you.

After three or four minutes, get together and discuss these questions:

- What are some words or names we associate with being proud? With being humble?

- Why do some words associated with pride have a more positive connotation in the secular worldview?

- Why do some words associated with humility have a more positive connotation in the Christian worldview?

Study It *(45-60 minutes)*

> If you have a large group, form smaller groups of four to seven people to answer the discussion questions. At the end of the Study It section, allow time for the subgroups to report to the whole group.

Read Isaiah 57:15 as well as the Dietrich Bonhoeffer quotation in the margin.

1. How would you define the type of humility that is appropriate for Christians to have? What kind of humility is inappropriate?

> "Only he who lives by the forgiveness of his sin in Jesus Christ will rightly think little of himself...Because the Christian can no longer fancy that he is wise he will also have no high opinion of his own schemes and plans."
>
> —**Dietrich Bonhoeffer**, *Life Together: A Discussion of Christian Fellowship*

2. What role does Jesus' forgiveness play in our humility? Why is humility before God both appropriate and necessary?

Read the Andrew Murray quotation in the margin.

3. In what sense is humility the highest virtue? How does humility, as defined by Murray, manifest itself in our actions and attitudes?

> "Humility, the place of entire dependence on God, is, from the very nature of things, the first duty and the highest virtue of the creature... And so pride, or the loss of this humility, is the root of every sin and evil."
>
> —**Andrew Murray**, *Humility: The Journey Toward Holiness*

Read Proverbs 16:18-19.

4. Do you agree that pride is the opposite of humility and that it's the root of every sin? Explain.

Read John 13:1-15.

5. How did Peter's pride almost prevent him from learning what Jesus was trying to teach him?

6. How has pride or a lack of humility gotten Christians and the church in trouble?

7. Form pairs or trios. Have each pair or trio look up one or
   two of the following Scripture passages and note what it
   teaches about humility. After three or four minutes, have each
   pair or trio summarize its passages and share insights with
   the rest of the group.

   - *1 Kings 3:5-9*
   - *Psalm 8:1-4*
   - *Psalm 131*
   - *Daniel 4:29-36*
   - *Matthew 18:1-4*
   - *Mark 10:42-45*

   - *Luke 14:7-11*
   - *Romans 12:3-5, 16*
   - *1 Corinthians 3:4-7*
   - *Galatians 6:3-4*
   - *Philippians 2:5-8*
   - *James 4:4-10*

8. What are the benefits of being humble before God and
   others?

9. In what ways do you find it to be a struggle to be truly
   humble? How can Christians develop the virtue of humility in
   their lives?

Close It *(15-30 minutes)*

Review the options in the Live It section of this session and make plans as a group to complete one of these activities prior to moving on to the next session. This is your opportunity to move from theory to practice—*carpe diem!*

Pray It

Share prayer requests and close in prayer. Be sure to ask God to guide your efforts as you plan and carry out a Live It activity.

Plan It

What activity are we going to do?

When are we doing this?

Where will this take place?

Other: special instructions/my responsibility

Part 2: live it

Option 1

John the Baptist said, "He [Christ] must become greater; I must become less" (John 3:30). Practice this verse this week. Spend this week serving others and God while being content to remain in the background humbly serving your Lord. This week, each time you are tempted to promote yourself in other's eyes through your words or actions, recite John 3:30 to yourself and resist the temptation. Give credit to others when it's due them, and let go of the resentment that sometimes comes from seeing others honored. Seek to tirelessly serve others with true Christian love. Think of others before yourself. Humbly submit to the leadership of your superiors and to your Lord. However, you must also resist the temptation to be falsely humble and either put yourself down or "fish" for compliments from others. Strive to find the balance between being confident of your position as a child of God and being a humble servant of God and others.

At the end of the week, meet with your small group to talk about your experiences. Talk about when you were able to be joyfully humble, and honestly confess when it was difficult. Pray together, asking God to help you learn what it means to be truly humble and selfless.

Option 2

Re-enact the Last Supper's foot-washing event as described in John 13:1-15. Have enough dishpans or large bowls on hand for people to pair off and take turns washing one another's feet. Be sure to have towels handy. Encourage the foot-washer to pray for the person whose feet are being washed. Come back together as a group to discuss how you felt on each side of the basin. Which was more humbling, being the washer or the "washee"? Explain your answers. Be sure to pray together, asking God to help you humbly serve one another daily with your words and your actions.

Option 3

Is there a child, co-worker, sibling, neighbor, parent, friend, or someone else whom you have offended through a harsh word, gossip, unfulfilled promise, or forgetfulness? The classic movie line "Love means never having to say you're sorry" is *not* true. Expressing regret for wronging another is both appropriate and necessary, but it isn't easy. Learning to sincerely say "I'm sorry" is an exercise in humility that can lead to a more loving relationship with the person offended. A contrite and humble heart helps us draw near to God and to others.

Ask God to bring to your mind someone who needs to hear you say, "I'm sorry." Offer an honest, heartfelt apology and ask to be forgiven. Express both your regret and your love and respect for the person. Don't put any conditions on your apology, and have no expectations of a response. Be prepared at your next meeting to relate your experience to the group and what you learned from it.

Option 4

Have everyone in the group commit to at least a two-hour block of time in the coming week to experience the world of the physically challenged together at a local mall or shopping center. Stay in pairs. Take turns limiting yourself physically by confining yourself to a wheelchair, by wearing a blackout blindfold, or by taping both thumbs to the palm of your hands. Learn what it's like to have to ask someone else for help, or to be completely dependent on someone else for the simplest of tasks, such as reaching something on a high shelf, getting a drink of water, or shopping for a shirt. For the more independent-minded, this can be a very humbling experience. What lessons about spiritual humility can you glean from this experience? Why do you think God wants us to have humble hearts? Then meet together in the food court for a snack and share your experiences with each other.

Option 5

Based on Luke 14:7-14, together plan a dinner for six to eight people and invite people who work in service professions as special

guests. Invite restaurant servers, day-care or nursing-home work-
ers, retail sales clerks, or people who clean homes or hotels. Set a
formal table—no plastic utensils or paper plates for this one. Treat
your guests as royalty, just as you would expect to be treated if
you were eating at a fancy restaurant. Be careful not to be conde-
scending. If they want to know why they are there, explain that
you are working on a lesson to learn a greater appreciation for
people whose jobs call for serving others. Talk to them about
their jobs and how those whom they serve treat them. Try as
much as possible to put yourselves in their shoes and learn from
them. See if this exercise changes your attitude the next time you
are impatient with a busy sales clerk or your waiter brings the
wrong meal to your table.

After the meal, discuss the event with the others in your small
group. See what lessons in humility you can glean both from your
humble service to your guests and also from your conversations
with them.

Debrief It

After experiencing this session's Live It activity, discuss these
questions as a group:

- **On a scale of 1 (low) to 10 (high), how would you
  rank this experience for yourself? Why?**

- **What was the most important insight you gained
  from this experience?**

- **How can you further develop this character trait?**

The following space is provided for you to record your personal thoughts, reflections, impressions, or feelings about this session's topic and Live It activity.

Contentment

When asked, "How much is enough?" many people answer, "A little bit more than I have right now." We live in a society that continually strives for more: more money, more time, more stuff. However, the Bible teaches that contentment is one of the marks of the mature Christian. In a predominantly materialistic world, the contented Christian stands out as one who has conquered the need to keep acquiring more things and seeking new, ever more exciting experiences, and is instead at peace with the circumstances of life, confident that God is taking care of all things.

The Bible doesn't require us to be hermits removed from this world, but rather demands a style of living that reflects Christ while we live in a sinful world. Imagine Jesus living next door to you today. What kind of lifestyle would Jesus pursue? What would we learn from his example? One thing would surely be a lifestyle of peaceful contentment. As Christians, we are called to follow Christ's example. We can show our transformed nature through a Christlike attitude of contentment.

Part 1: learn it

Start It *(15 minutes)*

Future/Past Perspective

Find a partner and talk about these questions:

- **What do you have today that you didn't have five, ten, or twenty-five years ago?**

- **Five, ten or twenty-five years ago, what did you think you'd have by now that you don't have?**

After five minutes of discussion, the leader will call time. With the whole group, discuss these questions:

- **In what ways is your life today different than you thought it would be?**

- **Do you think you're more or less content than you were in the past? Explain.**

Study It *(45-60 minutes)*

> If you have a large group, form smaller groups of four to seven people to answer the discussion questions. At the end of the Study It section, allow time for the subgroups to report to the whole group.

"True contentment is a thing as active as agriculture. It is the power of getting out of any situation all that there is in it. It is arduous and it is rare."

—G.K. Chesterton

Read the quotation in the margin. Also read Psalm 73:25-26; I Thessalonians 5:16-18; and Hebrews 13:5.

1. What do you think it means to be content as a Christian living in today's world? How does a contented person think and feel?

2. How do contented people act? approach decisions? face tough times? In what way is contentment "arduous"?

Read Matthew 6:19-21, 25-34.

3. Why does God want us to be content?

4. What difference would contented Christians make in today's world?

Read Philippians 4:11-13.

5. How is it possible to be content in all circumstances?

Read the margin quotation. Then compare I Timothy 6:6-8 with I Kings 10:8; Psalm 68:3; and Ecclesiastes 11:9.

6. What are the biggest barriers to contentment today?

7. How does a spirit of discontentment affect our lives? our witness in the world?

"Where am I responsible for my dissatisfaction? That question quickly led to others that revealed my expectations about life and my disappointment that it hadn't turned out as I'd hoped. Did my hopes and dreams spring *from God's promises*, or were they based on *my own ideas* about what I need?"

—Stephanie Peyton Barrett, "Journey to Contentment," Discipleship Journal, Issue 117

8. How can we overcome discontentment?

9. What specific steps can you take to nurture and retain a spirit of contentment in your life?

Close It *(15-30 minutes)*

Review the options in the Live It section of this session and make plans as a group to complete one of these activities prior to moving on to the next session. This is your opportunity to move from theory to practice—*carpe diem!*

Pray It

Share prayer requests and close in prayer. Be sure to ask God to guide your efforts as you plan and carry out a Live It activity.

Plan It

What activity are we going to do?

When are we doing this?

Where will this take place?

Other: special instructions/my responsibility

Part 2: live it

Option 1

During this coming week, count your blessings by keeping a journal of all the good things that happen to you. Also, list some of the things that you have that make life easier for you (for example, the car you drive to work) and thank God for each one as he reveals them to you. Gather together to share your insights with each other. Bring your journal and share some of the highlights from your week. Share how your perspective on contentment has changed throughout the week.

Have someone in the group acquire a copy of the book *Material World: A Global Family Portrait,* by Peter Menzel, Charles C. Mann, and Paul Kennedy, for you all to look through. The book features average families from thirty nations. The articles tell about each family's daily life. And each family is shown pictured outside their house surrounded by all of their possessions. Take at least an hour to look through the book and make observations and comparisons to your own lives.

Option 2

Have each person collect several pictures of starving children this week from magazines or the Internet. Put these pictures in several places where you'll encounter them throughout each day—for example, on the dining room table, next to your computer screen, in your car, in your Bible, or by your bedside. During the week, pay attention to the photos as you encounter them. Do all you can to make the children as real as possible. Study their cultures, pray for them, empathize with them. Contact agencies that feed starving children, and learn all you can about the children's plight. Write your feelings down on paper as you encounter the pictures throughout the week. Share your insights with the group at your next session. How did connecting with each of these children affect your thoughts about your own life? What did this teach you about contentment?

Option 3

Have each person in the group commit to a number of "no-spend" days during the upcoming week. Strive to commit to at least four no-spend days. On those days spend absolutely no money: Don't pay bills, don't buy gas, don't pick up a cup of coffee on the way to work, and don't pick up anything at the grocery store. Make do with what you have, and strive to be content without spending money. Notice how you feel during those days and whether the challenge to not spend money is easy or difficult. On the days that you do spend money, keep an accounting of every penny you spend. Note whether spending money makes you feel more content. Spend time in prayer, asking God to help you understand your feelings of discontentment and contentment. Perhaps there are attitudes and personal spending habits from which you need to repent.

At the end of the week, get together with the group for a no-spend social and share your triumphs and your challenges. Bring a treat made from items already in your pantry. Talk about what you've learned about money and contentment. Encourage each other to live according to your convictions and to be content with what you have.

Option 4

Challenge yourselves to each find fifty things in your home that you don't need. Give those items away to a Christian charity before the group meets again. Make a list of all the things you gave away. When you next meet, have everyone share their lists. What insights did you have as you considered what to give away and as you actually did give it away? Talk about whether it was easy or hard to give away your stuff. Talk about what you think the connection is between contentment and being attached to stuff. How much stuff do you need to be content? Challenge and encourage each other to be content and to have an appropriate attitude toward possessions. You may even want to challenge each other to give away another fifty things.

You may want to have everyone in your group gather all the giveaway items together and take them as a group to a Christian charity.

Option 5

In meetings of the Society of Friends (the Quakers), worshippers sit in silence, meditating until God gives them wisdom and insight. Such insight is shared with the entire group. Plan for a similar time of meditation on the Lord and his Word with your group. Gather everyone in a comfortable, quiet room. Print out Psalm 145:13-16 on a card for each person. Sit in silence for about thirty minutes and have everyone meditate on the verses, pray, and worship God.

To meditate, study each idea in the passage and ask God to give you insight. Sit silently and let God teach you. Some may want paper on which to record their insights; however, everyone should be encouraged to remain focused on God and Scripture during this time. Set a timer so that all in the group can focus on their meditation. At the end of the thirty minutes, talk about what God taught you.

Debrief It

After experiencing this session's Live It activity, discuss these questions as a group:

- **On a scale of 1 (low) to 10 (high), how would you rank this experience for yourself? Why?**

- **What was the most important insight you gained from this experience?**

- **How can you further develop this character trait?**

Journal It

The following space is provided for you to record your personal thoughts, reflections, impressions, or feelings about this session's topic and Live It activity.

Respect

R-E-S-P-E-C-T! The "Queen of Soul," Aretha
Franklin, sang about it, and the song she sang has
remained popular ever since. Perhaps the reason for its
popularity is that respect is indeed what most of us
want. We want to be treated as valuable, worthy people.
It seems natural to us to want to be *respected*, but being
respectful can be a little bit harder.

Our society focuses on the individual more than the
collective group. In a self-centered society, we seek to
promote, comfort, and care for ourselves before we look
to others. In some other cultures, where the emphasis is
on society rather than the individual, respect for others,
for institutions, and for the law is more common. Our
belief in Christ, however, leads us to an others-focused
perspective that is naturally respectful. Jesus taught us,
"So in everything, do to others what you would have
them do to you" (Matthew 7:12). Not only are we to be
respectful of others, we're to be respectful toward
authority, toward the law, and especially toward God.
This lesson will help you explore how to be respectful in
a way that pleases God.

Part 1: *learn it*

Start It *(15 minutes)*

Respectful Titles

> **Leader:** Have everyone in the group sit in a circle, so that each one in the group can clearly see every other person in the group.
> You'll need to have name tags and a pen available for this activity.

Have someone read the following paragraph aloud.

> Look around the group and think about what you have experienced together since the beginning of this study. What outstanding characteristics has each person shown? Together come up with a courtesy title for each person that says something about them. This title can be fun, but it should be respectful! For example, "Lady Chattey" might be cute for someone who delights your group with lively conversation, but "Lady Blabs-a-lot" would definitely not be respectful! "The Earl of Smiles" is a great title of respect for the person in the group with a good sense of humor. Write each person's new title on a name tag and have each person wear their name tag throughout the session.

When everyone has been given a respectful courtesy title, discuss the following questions:

- **What helps you feel respected in a group like this one?**

- **How do we show respect to each other in our society?**

For fun, call each other by title for the rest of today's session.

Study It *(45 minutes)*

1. What does it mean to be respectful? Why is it especially appropriate for Christians to be respectful?

2. In our society, what kinds of people, things, and institutions are respected? What kinds of people, things, and institutions aren't given respect?

> "Absolute respect for the person, the human being created by God—as a spiritual being who despite all his faults and wretchedness still retains something of God—will be the basis of a better civilization, and the foundation of better health for both individual and society. I always remember a remark that someone once made to me; 'In everyone I meet I try to see Jesus Christ.' "
>
> —Paul Tournier, *The Person Reborn*

Read the quotation from Paul Tournier.

3. What kind of difference would it make in the way we show respect to others if we all took this advice to see in everyone something of Jesus Christ?

4. In what way does mutual respect make for "the foundation of better health for both individual and society"?

Have two persons in the group read aloud the story of the Prodigal Son. Have one read Luke 15:11-24; and then have the other read the elder son's part of the story in Luke 15:25-32.

5. How did the younger son show a lack of respect for his father at the beginning of the story? Had he learned respect by the end? How about the elder son? Although he was more obedient, was he respectful?

6. The father calls for "the best robe," a ring, and sandals for his younger son when he returns. All of these would have commanded respect for the young man as the son of the landowner. What does this say to us about "earning" respect? Should a person have to do something to "earn" respect, or is it a gift of love?

7. Form pairs or trios. Have each pair or trio look up two or three of the following Scripture passages and note what they teach about being respectful. After three or four minutes, have the pairs or trios summarize their passages and share insights with the rest of the group.

- *Leviticus 19:3*
- *Leviticus 19:32*
- *Proverbs 11:16*
- *Malachi 1:6*
- *Romans 13:7*
- *Ephesians 5:33*

- *1 Thessalonians 5:12*
- *1 Timothy 3:4*
- *1 Peter 2:17*
- *1 Peter 3:7*
- *1 Peter 3:15*

Read the margin quotation.

8. Is it true that "we are losing even the appearance of courtesy" today, and if so, what is causing this to happen? How can we encourage talking to each other more respectfully?

"Now, when too many children run mad in the land, and now, when we need courtesy as much as or more than ever, and when a little tenderness between people could make life more bearable, we are losing even the appearance of courtesy. Our youth, finding little or no courtesy at home, make exodus into streets filled with violent self-revulsion and an exploding vulgarity."

—Maya Angelou, *Wouldn't Take Nothing for My Journey Now*

9. How can Christians develop a more respectful attitude? What will happen as a result of being more respectful?

Close It *(15-30 minutes)*

Review the options in the Live It section of this session and make plans as a group to complete one of these activities prior to moving on to the next session. This is your opportunity to move from theory to practice—*carpe diem!*

Pray It

Share prayer requests and close in prayer. Be sure to ask God to guide your efforts as you plan and carry out a Live It activity.

Plan It

What activity are we going to do?

When are we doing this?

Where will this take place?

Other: special instructions/my responsibility

Prayer Requests

Part 2: live it

Option 1

Created in the image of God, all human beings have dignity and are worthy of respect. However, many people live in oppression or without basic human rights and comforts. Show your respect for God's creation by promoting the cause of those who have no voice. Here are two ideas:

• Search Amnesty International's Web site (www.amnesty.org) to find human rights causes that you find compelling. Submit letters as guided in the Web site. You may want to follow the letter writing guidelines to draft your own letter rather than send the already-written letter the site provides. Together, discuss how writing letters shows respect for others.

• Search The Wilberforce Forum's Web site (www.wilberforce.org) to learn more about bioethics issues such as stem cell research, cloning, and abortion. Discuss ways you can show respect for people by getting involved in the bioethics debates. How would God have you show respect for those you disagree with? For those who cannot speak for themselves?

Option 2

As adults, it's not always easy to submit to the authority of others. Yet the Bible clearly instructs us to respect our leaders. This week, consider your attitudes toward all those in authority over you, including your boss, your pastor, and even elected officials. Choose someone from one of those categories and show them appropriate respect this week. Respect their leadership and their position. Remember that they were created by God and they are in authority over you because God gave them that authority. Consider how their God-given authority affects your attitude toward them, what you say about them, and how you respond to their leadership. You may need to adjust your attitude and your actions. However, remember that respect isn't the same as blind obedience. Think carefully about how you can disagree with a leader while still showing him or her respect.

At the end of the week, tell the rest of the group about your experiences. When was it difficult or easy to show sincere respect? Is it biblical to show respect when the other person's actions don't deserve respect? What did you learn through this experience?

Option 3

Gather to discuss respect within your small group. Set ground rules for your group. Perhaps you'll all agree to show respect to each other by arriving within five minutes of your agreed starting time, or perhaps you'll agree to leave by a certain time to respect your host or those who need to get up early the next morning. You may need to talk about committing to come each week out of respect for the one who prepares to facilitate each week's Bible study discussion. Talk about how to show respect for God's Word during your Bible studies. Also talk about how to respect each other when you disagree. Discuss how holding each other accountable and loving each other with sincere friendship are both part of respecting one another. What other ways of respecting each other can you find? You may need to spend some of your time confessing and asking one another for forgiveness. Be sure to end your time together in prayer, asking God to help you all love and respect each other sincerely.

Option 4

God's Word commands us to respect and honor our parents. Have each person in the group write a letter to his or her parents that shows honor and respect for them (you may want to gather together to work on the letters). For some, this may be a difficult or emotional exercise. Some parents have not behaved in a manner worthy of respect. Yet the biblical commandment remains. If someone in the group has had a difficult relationship with his or her parents, you may want to first spend time discussing how to appropriately show respect to someone who has hurt or wronged you. All people deserve respect as God's creations—no matter how wrong their actions.

Have everyone send their letters to their parents if they are able to. Those whose parents have died may simply want to thank God for their parents and honor their memory by sharing their letters with the rest of the small group.

Some adults may find that their attitudes toward their parents need to change and that their actions toward their parents need to be more respectful. Each person should prayerfully consider how to show their parents proper honor and respect. Meet together to talk about the experience and to share insights into respecting others.

Option 5

Show respect and honor for God this week by submitting to his authority as your Lord. Set your alarm fifteen minutes earlier than normal each day this week. After taking care of your personal needs, find a place in your house where you can be alone without distraction. If you have young children, try taking turns with your spouse. If you're a single parent, do this before your kids get up, or, if you have to, find another time during the day when you can be alone.

Prostrate yourself before the Lord (lie flat on your face) or kneel with head bowed. Tell God that you love him, that you recognize his authority and position as Lord of the universe, that you submit yourself to him, and that you commit the day with all its decisions and actions to him. Bring each concern of the day to God and leave it to him to deal with as he pleases. Recognize before God that his agenda, not yours, will be uppermost in your mind. State your intention to act today in a way that honors him. Take time to listen to God's instruction for the day. Praise God for his love and his gifts. End your prayer time by thanking God for the opportunity to serve him. Then be sure to fulfill your promises to God during the day!

At the end of the week, gather with your small group and talk about the experience. How did your prayers change your attitude toward God? How did your prayers change your actions?

Debrief It

After experiencing this week's Live It activity, discuss these questions as a group:

- **On a scale of 1 (low) to 10 (high), how would you rank this experience for yourself? Why?**

- **What was the most important insight you gained from this experience?**

- **How can you further develop this character trait?**

Journal It

The following space is provided for you to record your personal thoughts, reflections, impressions, or feelings about this session's topic and Live It activity.

Grace

It would have been enough if John Newton had stopped with writing the popular Christian hymn "Amazing Grace." This hymn captures the depth of gratitude Newton felt as a recipient of God's grace, and the song has encouraged millions of people in their friendship with God since it was written. But Newton didn't stop there. After his conversion, the former captain of a slave-trading ship tried to humanize the vocation by improving conditions on his ships and converting crew members. He couldn't even stop there. Newton quit his job, became a pastor, and continually spoke out against the slave trade.

The Lord's command to forgive as we have been forgiven is an overwhelming reminder that we don't have the right to seek revenge, to hate, or to withhold love. Once we have truly experienced grace, we have no choice but to extend it to others. The sacrifice that Jesus made for us while we were still "enemies of God" is so unmerited and so overwhelming, the only appropriate response is humble thanks, praise, and obedience. God's mercy and grace is so abundant and generous, how can we do anything less than show mercy, forgiveness, and grace to those who wrong us?

Start It *(15 minutes)*

This Is That

> If you have a large group, form groups of four to seven and have each group do this hands-on activity. Gather the group back together when it is time to discuss the questions.
>
> Leader: Tape three sheets of paper around the room. Test the sheets with a marker to make sure the marker doesn't bleed through to the walls. If it does, double up the sheets. Draw a vertical line down each sheet. On the top right of each sheet, write "Grace." On the top left of one sheet write "Judicial System." On the next sheet write "Competitive Sports" on the top left. On the third sheet write "Corporate World" on the top left.

Find a partner. Together, use the three sheets of paper to compare and contrast grace with various systems. For each of the systems, brainstorm a list of the following:

- **How does this system evaluate people?**

- **How does a person survive or win in this system?**

While you work, consider how grace compares to each system. For example, under the "Competitive Sports" column you might write, "Only takes the best." In the corresponding "Grace" column you might write, "Welcomes the best and worst."

When you're finished, or after five minutes, discuss the following questions with the entire group:

- **What is the biggest insight that you take away by looking at the lists you compiled?**

- **When you look at our society, in what way is grace a radical idea?**

- **When are people in this world likely to show grace? unlikely to show grace?**

Study It *(45-60 minutes)*

If you have a large group, form smaller groups of four to seven people to answer the discussion questions. At the end of the Study It section, allow time for the subgroups to report to the whole group.

1. Do you agree or disagree with the following statement: "Grace seems to be in short supply in the world today." Explain. Why are people hesitant to show grace to one another?

Read the quotation in the margin.

2. In what ways does grace defy logic? When have you experienced logic-defying grace?

3. Yancey borrows the term *grace-healed* eyes from the first-century theologian Irenaeus. How would you define *grace-healed* eyes? In what ways have your eyes been grace-healed? In what ways do you still need grace-healed eyes?

> "In this world we look up to the rich, the beautiful, the successful. Grace... introduces a world of new logic. Because God loves the poor, the suffering, the persecuted, so should we. Because God sees no undesirables, neither should we. Jesus challenged us to look at the world through...'grace-healed eyes.'"
>
> —Philip Yancey, *The Jesus I Never Knew*

Read the quotation in the margin.

4. How have Christians succeeded in following God's example of grace? How have Christians failed to follow God's example?

Read Matthew 7:1-5 and 18:21-35.

5. What happens when we're stingy with grace? when we're generous with grace?

6. Are people of grace pushovers? Explain. When is it appropriate to hold others accountable for their actions and when is it appropriate to extend grace?

7. How does our extending grace to others affect them? How does grace change the world?

8. Who do you know who needs more grace from you? How will you give it?

Close It *(15-30 minutes)*

Review the options in the Live It section of this session and make plans as a group to complete one of these activities prior to moving on to the next session. This is your opportunity to move from theory to practice—*carpe diem!*

Pray It

Share prayer requests and close in prayer. Be sure to ask God to guide your efforts as you plan and carry out a Live It activity.

Plan It

What activity are we going to do?

When are we doing this?

Where will this take place?

Other: special instructions/my responsibility

Part 2: live it

Option 1

Gather together for discussion, prayer, and commitment. Read the lyrics from the CD booklet to the song "Grace" by U2 (*All That You Can't Leave Behind*, Universal International Music). Then listen to the song together. Talk about how the song applies to your life or to the life of someone you know. Then read the words to "Amazing Grace" by John Newton (various recordings). Listen to the song together or, better yet, sing the song together. Talk about how the song applies to your life or the life of someone you know.

Then enter into a time of prayer. Ask God to help you make beauty out of ugly things, to be agents of God's grace in the world. Together, talk about your own community. Where in particular do you see a lack of grace? Where do hurting people encounter harsh judgment? Get involved in one of those areas and offer God's grace to hurting people. Here are some ideas of where you might start:
- at-risk youth or teenagers in your area's alternative high school
- children in the foster care system
- men or women in drug rehabilitation
- those suffering from HIV or AIDs
- youth in your area's juvenile detention facility

Option 2

For one full day, consider yourself to be a dispenser of grace. Offer grace to those who are rude, demanding, and selfish. Offer grace to those who hurt you, whether purposely or not. Offer grace to family, friends, and co-workers who fall short of your expectations. Offer grace to those who live contrarily to your values and beliefs.

During the day, consider the connections between grace, love, and compassion. Also consider how your perspective changes throughout the day. Consider whether you are truly offering grace if you must struggle to do so or find frustration and anger welling up within you. At the end of the day, praise God for the pure grace he offers to us. Offer yourself up to God and ask him to make you a more gracious, compassionate, and loving person.

When the group gets together again, talk about your experiences, your insights, your failures, and your growth. Encourage each other and pray together, asking God to help you be grace-full people.

Option 3

Extend grace to people who have encountered judgment. Prison Fellowship Ministries offers a variety of opportunities for your group to minister to prisoners, ex-prisoners, and their families. Opportunities include giving money, volunteering, and initiating awareness and fund-raising programs like Angel Tree. Study Prison Fellowship's ideas on restorative justice. See if you can adapt their ideas for use in your own community. You can connect with Prison Fellowship Ministries by visiting www.pfm.org, calling (877) 478-0100, or e-mailing correspondence@pfm.org. After your group decides how to volunteer, follow through!

Option 4

Gather together for a time of prayer. You'll need to plan about an hour for this activity. Make sure everyone in your group has an index card. Have everyone write "Second Chance List" at the top of their cards. Enter into a time of silent prayer. Have each person prayerfully consider people they need to forgive or give a second chance to. Everyone should list names or initials on their cards. The participants can pray about each person and each situation, asking God's help to forgive. Then everyone should choose to forgive. Have everyone pray that God would help and bless the people on their lists, and then look for ways to show God's love to those people in practical and real ways.

Option 5

It's impossible for us to extend grace to others when we haven't experienced or accepted God's grace ourselves. Talk to a trusted friend in this group about something you've done or experienced that you feel has not been touched by the grace of God. Be completely open about what happened, bringing the entire situation to light, and let God's perfect, redemptive grace cover you. Ask your friend to pray with you and for you. Then memorize this verse: "From the fullness of his grace we have all received one blessing after another" (John 1:16). Spend much time dwelling on the fullness of God's grace and the blessings you've received from him.

The next time the group meets, let them know about your progress. You don't have to give details; just let the group hold you accountable to praying with your trusted friend and allowing God to shed his grace on every part of your life.

Debrief It

After experiencing this session's Live It activity, discuss these questions as a group:

- **On a scale of 1 (low) to 10 (high), how would you rank this experience for yourself? Why?**

- **What was the most important insight you gained from this experience?**

- **How can you further develop this character trait?**

Journal It

The following space is provided for you to record your personal thoughts, reflections, impressions, or feelings about this session's topic and Live It activity.

Learn It, Live It Bible Studies®:
Christian Character

Please help Group Publishing, Inc., continue to provide innovative and useful resources for ministry. Please take a moment to fill out this evaluation and mail or fax it to us. Thanks!

Group Publishing, Inc.
Attention: Product Development
P.O. Box 481
Loveland, CO 80539
Fax: (970) 292-4370

1. As a whole, this book has been (circle one)
   not very helpful   *very helpful*
   1   2   3   4   5   6   7   8   9   10

2. The best things about this book:

3. Ways this book could be improved:

4. Things I will change because of this book:

5. Other books I'd like to see Group publish in the future:

6. Would you be interested in field-testing future Group products and giving us your feedback? If so, please fill in the information below:

Name_____

Church Name _____

Denomination _____ Church Size _____

Church Address _____

City _____ State_____ ZIP _____

Church Phone _____

E-mail _____

that everyone craves.

that really matters.

that gets undivided attention.

that can transform your life.

that encourages pastors.

that will re-energize you.

that will bring you joy.

that will unite your community.

that brings families closer.

that frees you.

that gives you focus.

that answers the why's.

that means true success.

that eliminates distractions.

that gives you real purpose.

the 1 thing™ that can transform your church.

Discover how *The 1 Thing* can revolutionize the way you approach ministry. It's engaging. Fun. Even shocking. But most of all, it's about re-thinking what "growing a relationship with Jesus" really means. Pick up Thom & Joani Schultz's inspiring new book today.

Thom & Joani Schultz

the 1 thing

*What everyone craves—
that your church can deliver*

More Life-Changing Ideas for Your Adult Ministry

from Group Publishing…

God's Good Gifts

A Scrapbooking Bible Study for Women's Groups

Devotions from…
Kay Arthur
Emilie Barnes
Jill Briscoe
Jody Brolsma
Sherri Harris
Amy Nappa

the **1** thing™